What Would You Do?

by Jane Belk Moncure
illustrated by
Kathryn Hutton

Published by The Dandelion House
A Division of The Child's World

for distribution by **VICTOR**
BOOKS a division of SP Publications, Inc.
WHEATON. ILLINOIS 60187

Offices also in
Whitby, Ontario, Canada
Amersham-on-the-Hill, Bucks, England

Published by The Dandelion House, A Division of The Child's World, Inc.
© 1985 SP Publications, Inc. All rights reserved. Printed in U.S.A.

A Book for Preschoolers.

Library of Congress Cataloging in Publication Data

Moncure, Jane Belk.
  What would you do?

  Summary: Presents, in brief text and illustrations,
a variety of familiar situations involving such concepts
as sharing, being responsible, and being kind and
encourages the reader to decide on the appropriate
behavior.
    1. Children—Conduct of life.   [1. Behavior.
2. Conduct of life.   3. Decision making]   I. Hutton,
Kathryn, ill.   II. Title.   III. Series.
BJ1631.M684   1985   170'.2'0222   85-10418
ISBN 0-89693-227-3

1 2 3 4 5 6 7 8 9 10 11 12 R 91 90 89 88 87 86 85

What Would You Do?

"Do to others as you would have them do to you."
—Luke 6:31 (NIV)

Ann sees an empty swing on the
playground. She runs to get on it,

but Tommy gets there first.

What does Ann do? Does she
pull it away and jump on, or . . .

. . . does she say, "My turn next?"
If you were there too,
what would you do?

Rosita climbs to the top of the slide.
She stands there, afraid to go down.
Heather is right behind her, waiting.
What does Heather do?

Does Heather say, "Hurry up, Rosita,"
and push her down the slide? Or,
does she say, "That's okay! Do you
want me to go first and show you how?"

    If you were there too,
what would you do?

Laura has a knot in her shoestring.
She has been trying and trying to get
it untied. Now she pulls and kicks off
her shoe, just as Jill comes by.

What does Jill do? Does she laugh
and make fun of Laura?

Is there a better way?
What would you say?

11

Mom calls from upstairs, "Be sure to wear your boots when you go out- side in the snow."

Tim looks in the closet, but his boots are not there. What does he do?

Does he run outside without his boots? Or, does he look until he finds them?

If you were there too, what would you do?

Brad is building a church with blocks.
He is putting on the steeple when Mike
walks too close, touches the blocks,
and down they tumble.

Does Mike pretend he didn't touch them and walk by? Or, does he say, "Oops, I'm sorry!" and help build the church again?

What happens next with these two? If you were there, what would you do?

Mai and Stephanie are playing house.
Melinda wants to play too.

Do Mai and Stephanie tell her there
isn't room? Or, do they let her come in?
Can you help the two girls
decide what to do?

Josh and Ron walk by Jason's house.
Jason is sitting all alone—without
a friend.

Do they just wave? Or, do they say,
"Come on, Jason. We need you on
our baseball team."

Can you help the two?
What would you do?

Eddie is playing in the sandbox with
his little brother, Ben.

Ben throws sand. Where does it land?
In Eddie's hair! What does Eddie do?
Does he throw sand too? Or . . .

. . . does he say, "Stop! Sand belongs
in the sandbox, not in people's hair!"

What would you do
if you were there?

Melissa and Omee want to play with the
same doll. "I want her," says Melissa.
"No, I do," says Omee.

They push and pinch and shout!

What happens now? Do they call
each other names? Do they stop
being friends?

Can they work things out?
Can you tell them how?

Todd finds some money on the playground. What does he do? Does he put it in his pocket and say, "Finders keepers"?

Can you tell Todd what you would
do with something that didn't belong
to you?

Suzanne's sister is sick and can't go
outside to play. Mother stays with her
all day. When Daddy comes home, he
reads her a story. Suzanne feels left
out. Does she hug Teddy and pout?

Or, does she find a special way to make
her sister feel better today?

Let's go through each day,
remembering to treat others
as we want them to treat us.